The Ultimate Cheesecake Recipe Book

Delicious, Creamy Cheesecake Recipes That Everyone Will Love!

BY: Allie Allen

COOK & ENJOY

Copyright 2020 Allie Allen

Copyright Notes

This book is written as an informational tool. While the author has taken every precaution to ensure the accuracy of the information provided therein, the reader is warned that they assume all risk when following the content. The author will not be held responsible for any damages that may occur as a result of the readers' actions.

The author does not give permission to reproduce this book in any form, including but not limited to: print, social media posts, electronic copies or photocopies, unless permission is expressly given in writing.

Table of Contents

Introduction 6

    Chocolate Cheesecake 7

    Oreo Cheesecake 10

    Nutella Oreo Cheesecake 13

    Peanut Butter Cup Cheesecake 16

    Berry-Ricotta Cheesecake 20

    Pumpkin Cheesecake 23

    White Chocolate Raspberry Swirl Cheesecake 28

    Carrot Cake Cheesecake 31

    Classic Cheesecake 34

    Biscoff Cheesecake 36

    Lemon Cheesecake 38

    Orange Cheesecake 41

    Raspberry Cheesecake Pie 44

    Mandarin Orange Cheesecake 46

Chocolate Quark Cheesecake 49

Red Velvet Cheesecake 53

Banana Cream Cheesecake 57

White Chocolate Cheesecake 60

Black Forest Cheesecake 62

Ricotta Pineapple Cheesecake 64

Fruit Cheesecake Pie 66

White Chocolate Oreo Cheesecake 69

Blue Velvet Cheesecake 72

Peaches and Cream Cheesecake 76

Matcha Cheesecake 78

Lavender Cheesecake 81

Mango Cheesecake 84

Caramel Cheesecake 87

Chocolate Mocha Cheesecake 90

Caramel Coffee Cheesecake 93

Conclusion 96

About the Author 97

Author's Afterthoughts 99

Introduction

Are you looking to create the perfect cheesecake at home but don't know where to begin? Look no further than this recipe book! Filled with delicious cheesecake recipes varying from the classics to bolder flavors, there's something in here that will appeal to everyone!

Plus, all of the recipes in this book are simple and pretty straight-forward, making it perfect for even the most beginner of bakers! So what are you waiting for? Choose a cheesecake recipe, and let's get started!

Chocolate Cheesecake

An insanely delicious, rich, moist, and dense chocolate cheesecake that you won't be able to get enough of.

Makes: 8 – 12 servings

Prep: 15 mins

Cook: 1 hr. plus cooling time

Ingredients:

For the Crust:

- 12 Oreo cookies, crushed, plus extra to serve
- 1 tbsp. white sugar
- 2 tbsp. unsalted butter, melted

For the Filling:

- 4 tbsp. milk
- 1 cup semisweet chocolate chips
- ½ tsp. espresso powder
- 12 oz. cream cheese, softened
- 1/2 cup white sugar
- 2 large eggs
- ½ tsp. vanilla extract
- 1 tbsp. flour

Directions:

Preheat the oven to 375F & slightly grease a 6"inch springform pan.

For the Crust: In a medium-sized bowl, combine the crushed Oreos, sugar & melted butter. Press the crumb mixture in pan & bake for 10 minutes. Remove & set aside to slightly cool.

Reduce the oven to 350°F.

For filling: In a saucepan, combine the milk and chocolate chips and heat on low until the chocolate chips are melted. Remove from heat and add in the espresso powder. Set the mixture aside.

In a large bowl, beat together the cream cheese and sugar for about 2 minutes. Add in the eggs & beat again until well-combined. Finally, add in the vanilla extract and flour and beat until well-combined.

Pour batter onto the crust then bake for about 45 minutes or until a toothpick placed into the edge of the cake comes out clean.

Turn off the oven and, leave the door open several inches and leave to cool for about an hour.

Remove, cover and cool in the refrigerator for another hour or until ready to serve.

Top with crushed Oreos and serve.

Enjoy!

Oreo Cheesecake

This light, creamy and easy cheesecake recipe comes with a delicious Oreo base and requires no baking whatsoever.

Makes: 10 servings

Prep: 5 hrs. 25 mins

Cook: -

Ingredients:

For the Crust:

- 25 Oreos
- ¼ cup unsalted butter, melted

For the cheesecake:

- 16 oz. cream cheese, softened
- 1 cup icing sugar
- 1 tsp. vanilla extract
- 1 cup heavy whipping cream, cold
- 14 Oreos, chopped, plus extra for topping

Directions:

For the Crust:

Place Oreos in a food processor & process to crumbs. Transfer to a bowl, add in the melted butter and mix until combined.

Scoop the mixture into a 9-inch springform pan and press until even. Place in the fridge to chill.

For the cheesecake:

In a bowl, using a hand mixer/stand mixer, beat the cream cheese for 1 minute or until smooth. Add in the icing sugar and vanilla and beat until well combined.

In a med-sized bowl, beat the heavy cream for 3 minutes. Fold it in to the cream cheese until just combined. Lastly, fold in the chopped Oreos.

Remove the pan from the fridge, pour in the cream cheese mixture and using a spatula, spread it around evenly. Sprinkle on additional chopped Oreos and press them slightly into the cheesecake.

Cover & refrigerate for 5 hrs. or overnight.

Enjoy!

Nutella Oreo Cheesecake

A heavenly Nutella cheesecake recipe that is a cinch to prepare.

Makes: 8 – 12 servings

Prep: 15 mins

Cook: 1 hr. plus cooling time

Ingredients:

For the Crust:

- 12 Oreo cookies, crushed, plus extra to serve
- 1 tbsp. white sugar
- 2 tbsp. unsalted butter, melted

For the Filling:

- 4 tbsp. milk
- 1 cup Nutella
- ½ tsp. espresso powder
- 12 oz. cream cheese, softened
- 1/2 cup white sugar
- 2 large eggs
- ½ tsp. vanilla extract
- 1 tbsp. flour

Directions:

Preheat the oven to 375F & slightly grease a 6"inch springform pan.

For the Crust: In a medium-sized bowl, combine the crushed Oreos, sugar & melted butter. Press the crumb mixture in pan & bake for 10 minutes. Remove & set aside to slightly cool.

Reduce the oven to 350°F.

For Filling: In a saucepan, combine the milk and Nutella and heat on low until the chocolate chips are melted. Remove from heat and add in the espresso powder. Set the mixture aside.

In a large bowl, beat together the cream cheese and sugar for about 2 minutes. Add in the eggs & beat again until well-combined. Finally, add in the vanilla extract and flour and beat until well-combined.

Pour batter onto the crust and bake for about 45 minutes or until a toothpick placed into the edge of the cake comes out clean.

Turn off the oven and, leave the door open several inches and leave to cool for about an hour.

Remove, cover and cool in the refrigerator for another hour or until ready to serve.

Top with crushed Oreos and serve.

Enjoy!

Peanut Butter Cup Cheesecake

A rich and creamy cheesecake where the crust is a combination of sandwich-cookie crumbs, graham cracker crumbs, and peanut butter. The gooey cheesecake is filled with cream cheese, sour cream, and vanilla; garnished with ice cream topping with peanut butter cups.

Makes: 16 servings

Prep: 1hr plus cooling time

Cook: 65 mins

Ingredients:

Crust:

- 3/4 cup creamy peanut butter
- 1 1/2 cup graham cracker crumbs
- 1/4 cup sugar
- 6 tablespoons butter
- 1/4 cup finely crushed chocolate sandwich-cookie crumbs

Cheesecake:

- Peanut butter cups
- 1 cup sugar
- 3 eggs
- 3 packages cream cheese
- 1 cup sour cream
- 1 cup of hot fudge topping (ice cream)
- 1 1/2 teaspoon vanilla extract

Directions:

Crust:

Preheat oven to 350 Fahrenheit.

Brush with melted butter a nine-inch springform pan.

Combine in a large bowl the cookie crumbs, 6 tablespoons sugar and butter.

Line the bottom of pan with the crust with one inch up the side of the pan. Bake for ten minutes until set. Let cool on the wire rack.

Place in a small bowl the peanut butter and microwave on high thirty seconds until melted. Then, brush melted peanut into the bottom of the crust.

Cheesecake:

Beat on medium speed the sugar and cream cheese in a large bowl with mixer for three minutes until smooth. Scrape down the sides with rubber spatula.

Beat in vanilla and sour cream. Beat eggs on low speed until blended completely. Reserve one cup of batter. Fill the crust with the remainder of the creamy batter into the prepared crust.

Microwave on high thirty seconds, in a small bowl, the one-fourth of the hot fudge topping until the mixture is pourable.

Fold hot fudge topping into the reserved batter.

Slowly pour the chocolate filling over the batter in the springform pan and swirl with a knife.

Put the springform pan in the pan on the oven rack. Slowly, fill the roasting pan with hot water at least halfway up the side of the springform pan.

Bake the cake for fifty-five minutes until the edges are set and the center is wobbly. Turn off the oven. Remove the springform pan from the pan.

Place the springform pan again in the oven to cool naturally, with the door slightly open for two hours. Let cool in a wire rack.

Place in a small bowl the remainder of the hot fudge topping and microwave on high thirty seconds in the microwave until pourable.

Frost the top using an offset spatula. Let cool and arrange on top with peanut butter cups.

Cover the cake and refrigerate for six hours to three days until ready to serve.

Serve!

Berry-Ricotta Cheesecake

Finish your dinner with a bite of this lovely cheesecake topped with berries and confectioner's sugar. You can't ever go wrong with this velvety, lemony, zesty, creamy, and cheesy Berry-Ricotta Cheesecake.

Makes: 16 servings

Prep: 1 hr.

Cook: 1 hr.

Ingredients:

- 1 1/2 cup graham cracker crumbs
- 6 tablespoons butter (margarine)
- 1 1/2 cup granulated sugar
- 1 tablespoon of granulated sugar
- 2 lemons
- 15 ounces ricotta cheese
- 16 ounces reduced-fat cream cheese (Neufchatel)
- 2 cups half-and-half
- 2 teaspoons vanilla extract
- 3 tablespoons cornstarch
- 1 teaspoon almond extract
- 4 large eggs
- 1 tablespoon confectioners' sugar
- 2 1/2 cups mixed berries

Directions:

Preheat oven at 375 degrees Fahrenheit.

Cover with a heavy-duty foil the exterior part a nine-inch springform pan to prevent leakage. Spray the pan with cooking spray.

Combine in a medium bowl the butter, 1 tablespoon of granulated sugar and butter. Press the mixture firmly on the bottom of the springform pan.

Bake the crust for 8-10 mins until the edge is browned. Let cool on wire rack. Reduce oven temperature to 325 degrees Fahrenheit.

Meanwhile, grate from lemon fruit one tablespoon peel and squeeze out at least one-fourth cup of juice, set aside.

Beat in a bowl of a mixer the ricotta cheese and the reduced-fat cream cheese on high speed until smooth.

Beat in cornstarch, ¼ teaspoon salt and 1 ½ cups of granulated sugar. Scrape the sides of the bowl with a rubber spatula; continue beating on low speed until fully blended.

Add half-and-half, almond extracts, and vanilla and beat on low speed, add the lemon juice and lemon peel. Beat in eggs until all ingredients are blended well.

Fill the crust with the batter and bake for one hour. Turn off oven & leave the cake stand in oven for one hour.

Loosen the edge of cake by running a knife. Cool in a pan rack for one hour before covering and placing in refrigerator for six hours until two days.

Spread berries on top of the cheesecake. Spread confectioner's sugar on the berries through a sieve.

Serve!

Pumpkin Cheesecake

This cake is baked in a water bath to retain the natural flavor of the pumpkin. This light textured cheesecake is adorned with sugared cranberries, after spreading the rich-flavored sour-cream topping.

Makes: 16 servings

Prep: 2 hrs. plus overnight

Cook: 1 hr.

Ingredients:

Crumb Crust:

- 2 tablespoons sugar
- 3 tablespoons melted butter
- 1 cup graham-cracker crumbs

Pumpkin Cheesecake Filling:

- 1 1/4 cup granulated sugar
- 2 (8 ounces) packages softened cream cheese
- 1 (15 ounces) can pure pumpkin
- 3/4 cup sour cream
- 2 teaspoons
- 1 teaspoon ground cinnamon
- 4 large eggs
- 1/2 teaspoon ground allspice
- 1/4 teaspoon salt

Sour-Cream Topping:

- 3 tablespoons granulated sugar
- 1 1/3 cups sour cream
- 1 teaspoon vanilla extract

Sugared Cranberries:

- 1/2 cup cranberries
- 1/2 cup granulated sugar
- 3 tablespoons light corn syrup
- Note: This recipe requires you to use pure pumpkin and not pumpkin-pie mix.

Directions:

Preheat the oven at 350 degrees Fahrenheit.

Stir in a 9x3-inch springform pan with a fork the graham-cracker crumbs with the sugar.

Stir in melted butter until moistened. Press the mixture with your fingers on the bottom of springform pan.

Wrap with a heavy-duty foil the exterior part of the pan to avoid leaking out during the baking process in water bath.

Bake the crust for ten minutes and let cool in pan on the wire rack.

Pumpkin Cheesecake Filling:

Beat on medium speed in a large bowl with mixer the cream cheese, until the texture turns smooth.

Gradually add and beat the sugar for one minute until well blended while scraping often the sides of the bowl with spatula.

Beat at low speed with a mixer the sour cream, vanilla extract or bourbon, pumpkin, allspice, salt and cinnamon.

Add individual eggs and beat immediately after every addition until well blended.

Fill the crust with the mixture & put in a large roasting pan.

Position the pan on your oven rack. Slowly pour boiling water about 1 inch depth enough to cover the side of the springform pan.

Bake the cheesecake for one hour until lightly browned and there is no more movement in the center of cake.

Sour-Cream Topping:

Whisk with a wire whisk in a small bowl the vanilla, sour cream and sugar until incorporated.

Remove the springform pan from the oven and spread the sour cream topping over the cake.

Put back the pan to the oven and bake for an additional seven minutes.

Remove the cake from the water bath and transfer to a wire rack. Remove and discard the foil.

Make the sides lose by running a butter knife around the sides, slowly to prevent cracking.

Let cake cool completely. Cover with plastic & chill for six hours or overnight.

Sugared Cranberries:

Meanwhile, put one-half cup of sugar on a waxed paper sheet.

Heat in a saucepan the corn syrup and bring to a boil. Stir in cranberries for one minute.

Remove saucepan from heat. Transfer the cranberries from the pan to the waxed paper.

Roll cranberries until thoroughly coated with sugar. Let cranberries dry.

Garnish the cheesecake with sugar-coated cranberries.

Enjoy!

White Chocolate Raspberry Swirl Cheesecake

This cheesecake is one of Cheesecake Factory's most popular desserts. This recipe is inspired by that luscious creamy cake.

Makes: 10 servings

Prep: 45 mins plus 5 hrs.

Cook: 1 hr. 15 mins

Ingredients:

Crust

- ⅓ cup butter, melted
- 1 ½ cups chocolate cookie crumbs, such as crumbled Oreo® cookies

Filling

- 1 ¼ cups granulated sugar
- 4 ounces white chocolate, chopped into chunks
- 4 (8-ounce) packages cream cheese
- 2 teaspoons vanilla extract
- ½ cup sour cream
- ½ cup raspberry preserves (or raspberry pie filling)
- ¼ cup water
- 5 eggs

Optional Garnish

- 2 ounces shaved white chocolate (optional)
- Fresh whipped cream

Directions:

Preheat the oven to 475°F.

In a food processor, crumble the cookies and add the melted butter. Press the mixture into a greased 9-inch springform pan, and place in the freezer while you make the filling.

Pour half an inch of water in a large baking pan (it needs to fit your springform pan) and place it in the oven.

In a mixing bowl, beat together the cream cheese, sugar, sour cream, and vanilla.

Beat the eggs & then add them slowly to the cream cheese mixture.

In another small dish, mix the raspberry preserves and water. Microwave for 1 minute.

Remove the crust from the freezer & cover the outside bottom of the pan with aluminum foil. Sprinkle the white chocolate over the crust, then pour half of the cheesecake batter into the springform pan. Next, drizzle half of the raspberry preserves over the top of the batter. Then add the rest of the batter with the rest of the drizzle.

Place the pan into the water bath & bake for 15 minutes at 475°F, then reduce heat to 350F & bake about 60 more minutes more, or until the center is set & cake is cooked through.

Remove from oven & cool it completely before removing sides of pan, then move to the refrigerator for at least 5 hours.

Serve with extra white chocolate and fresh whipped cream.

Carrot Cake Cheesecake

What do you get when you combine carrot cake with cheesecake? This delicious recipe!

Makes: 12 servings

Prep: 20 mins plus 5 hrs.

Cook: 1 hr.

Ingredients:

Cheesecake:

- 1 teaspoon vanilla
- 3 eggs
- 1 tablespoon flour
- 2 (8-ounce) blocks cream cheese, room temperature
- ¾ cup sugar

Carrot Cake:

- ¾ cup vegetable oil
- 1 teaspoon vanilla
- 1 cup sugar
- 1 teaspoon cinnamon
- 2 eggs
- 1 cup flour
- ½ cup flaked coconut
- 1 teaspoon baking soda
- 1 dash salt
- ½ cup chopped walnuts
- 1 (8-oz) can crushed pineapple, well drained with juice kept aside
- 1 cup grated carrot

Pineapple Cream Cheese Frosting:

- 1 ¾ cups powdered sugar
- 2 ounces cream cheese, softened
- ½ teaspoon vanilla
- 1 tablespoon butter, softened
- 1 tablespoon reserved pineapple juice

Directions:

Preheat oven to 350F & grease a 9-inch springform pan.

In a bowl, beat cream cheese & the sugar until smooth. Then beat in the flour, eggs, and vanilla until well combined. Set aside.

In another large bowl, beat together the ¾ cup vegetable oil, sugar, eggs and vanilla until smooth. Then add the flour, baking soda, cinnamon and salt and beat until smooth. Fold in the crushed pineapple, grated carrot, coconut, and walnuts.

Pour 1 ½ cups of the carrot cake batter into the prepared pan. Drop spoonfuls of the cream cheese batter on the top of the carrot cake batter. Then add spoonfuls of carrot cake batter over the top of the cream cheese batter. Repeat with the remaining batter.

Bake for 50–60 mins. Remove & cool for about an hour before taking the sides off the springform pan. Refrigerate for at least 5 hours.

Beating together all the frosting ingredients. Frost the cake when it is completely cold.

Classic Cheesecake

A delicious classic cheesecake that's creamy and addicting!

Makes: 12 servings

Prep: 4 hrs. 15 mins

Cook: 1 hr. 5 mins

Ingredients:

Crust:

- ⅓ cup margarine, melted
- ¼ teaspoon ground cinnamon
- 1 ½ cups graham cracker crumbs

Filling:

- 2 teaspoons vanilla extract
- ½ cup sour cream
- 5 large eggs
- 1 ¼ cups white sugar
- 4 (8-ounce) packages cream cheese, softened

Topping:

- ½ cup sour cream
- 2 teaspoons sugar

Directions:

Preheat oven to 475F & place a skillet with half an inch of water inside.

Combine the ingredients for crust in a bowl. Line a large pie pan with a parchment paper and spread crust onto pan. Press firmly. Cover it with foil & keep it in the freezer until ready to use.

Combine all for filling apart from the eggs in a bowl. . Mix in eggs 1 at a time & beat until fully blended.

Remove the crust & pour in the filling, spreading it evenly. Place the pie pan into the heated skillet in the oven and bake for about 12 minutes.

Reduce the heat to 350°F. Continue to bake for about 50 minutes, or until the top of the cake is golden. Remove it from the oven & move the skillet onto a wire rack to cool.

Prepare the topping by mixing all ingredients in a bowl. Coat the cake with the topping, then cover. Refrigerate for at least 4 hours.

Serve cold.

Biscoff Cheesecake

This light, creamy, and easy cheesecake recipe comes with a delicious Lotus biscuit base and requires no baking whatsoever.

Makes: 10 servings

Prep: 5 hrs. 25 mins

Cook: -

Ingredients:

For the Crust:

- Place Lotus cookies in a food processor and process to crumbs. Transfer to a bowl,
- add in the melted butter and mix until combined.
- Scoop the mixture into a 9-inch springform pan and press until even. Place in the
- fridge to chill.

For the cheesecake:

In a bowl, using a hand mixer/stand mixer, beat the cream cheese for 1 minute or until smooth. Add in the icing sugar and vanilla and beat until well combined.

In a med-sized bowl, beat the heavy cream for 3 minutes. Fold it in to the cream cheese until just combined. Lastly, fold in the chopped cookies.

Remove the pan from the fridge, pour in the cream cheese mixture and using a spatula, spread it around evenly. Sprinkle on additional chopped Lotus biscuits and press them slightly into the cheesecake.

Cover & refrigerate for 5 hrs. or overnight.

Enjoy!

Lemon Cheesecake

A delicious lemon cheesecake that's zesty, light, and absolutely scrumptious!

Makes: 12 servings

Prep: 4 hrs. 15 mins

Cook: 1 hr. 5 mins

Ingredients:

Crust:

- ⅓ cup margarine, melted
- ¼ teaspoon ground cinnamon
- 1 ½ cups graham cracker crumbs

Filling:

- ½ cup sour cream
- 4 (8-ounce) packages cream cheese, softened
- 2 teaspoons vanilla extract
- 1 ¼ cups white sugar
- Zest of 1 lemon
- Juice of 2 lemons
- 5 large eggs

Directions:

Preheat oven to 475F & place a skillet with half an inch of water inside.

Combine the ingredients for crust in a bowl. Line a large pie pan with parchment paper and spread crust onto pan. Press firmly. Cover it with foil & keep it in the freezer until ready to use.

Combine all for filling apart from the eggs in a bowl. Mix in eggs 1 at a time & beat until fully blended.

Remove the crust & pour in the filling, spreading it evenly. Place the pie pan into the heated skillet in the oven and bake for about 12 minutes.

Reduce the heat to 350°F. Continue to bake for about 50 minutes, or until the top of the cake is golden. Remove it from the oven & move the skillet onto a wire rack to cool.

Refrigerate for at least 4 hours.

Serve cold.

Orange Cheesecake

An amazing orange cheesecake recipe that's super simple and delicious!

Makes: 12 servings

Prep: 4 hrs. 15 mins

Cook: 1 hr. 5 mins

Ingredients:

Crust:

- ⅓ cup margarine, melted
- ¼ teaspoon ground cinnamon
- 1 ½ cups graham cracker crumbs

Filling:

- ½ cup sour cream
- 4 (8-ounce) packages cream cheese, softened
- 2 teaspoons vanilla extract
- 1 ¼ cups white sugar
- Zest of 2 oranges
- 5 large eggs

Directions:

Preheat oven to 475F & place a skillet with half an inch of water inside.

Combine the ingredients for crust in a bowl. Line a large pie pan with parchment paper and spread crust onto pan. Press firmly. Cover it with foil & keep it in the freezer until ready to use.

Combine all for filling apart from the eggs in a bowl. Mix in eggs 1 at a time & beat until fully blended.

Remove the crust & pour in the filling, spreading it evenly. Place the pie pan into the heated skillet in the oven and bake for about 12 minutes.

Reduce the heat to 350°F. Continue to bake for about 50 minutes, or until the top of the cake is golden. Remove it from the oven & move the skillet onto a wire rack to cool.

Refrigerate for at least 4 hours.

Serve cold.

Raspberry Cheesecake Pie

A delicious cross between a cheesecake and pie.

Makes: 9 servings

Prep: 15 mins

Cook: 1 hr.

Ingredients:

- 2 tbsp. raspberry jam
- 1 × baked sweet shortcrust pastry case, in an 8in square
- Baking tin/ovenproof dish
- 3 tbsp. plain flour
- 1½ lb. cream cheese
- 3½oz double cream
- 4 large eggs, beaten
- 200g (7oz) light muscovado sugar
- 2 tsp vanilla paste/extract
- Grated zest of 1 lemon
- 1 tbsp. cornflour
- 5oz fresh raspberries

Directions:

Preheat the oven to 325°F.

Spread the jam at the bottom of cooked pastry case.

In a bowl, mix the cream cheese with the cream. Add in the eggs, then the sugar, zest and vanilla.

Fold in the flours, & then pour the mixture into the pastry case on top of the jam. Put the raspberries into the filling.

Bake for 1 hr., then turn the oven off & leave to cool inside, with the door ajar. Leave in the dish and place in the refrigerator to set for at least 1 hour before serving.

Mandarin Orange Cheesecake

A delicious zesty cheesecake recipe that citrus lovers will love!

Makes: 8 servings

Prep: 1 hr.

Cook: 30 mins

Ingredients:

Crust

- 1½ cups, scooped and leveled/190g all-purpose flour
- 1 teaspoon baking powder
- ¼ cup/50g granulated sugar
- Pinch of salt
- 1 egg
- 7 tablespoons/100g unsalted high-fat, European-style butter, at room temperature, cubed

Filling

- 1 cup/200g granulated sugar
- 4 eggs
- ⅓ cup plus 1 teaspoon/50g cornstarch
- ⅛ teaspoon salt
- 4 cups/1kg Quark, drained if necessary (see this page)
- ½ cup/120g sour cream
- 1¼ teaspoons vanilla extract
- ½ cup/120ml neutral vegetable oil
- ½ cup/120ml milk
- 2 (11-ounce/310g) cans mandarin oranges, drained

Directions:

For crust: In a bowl, mix together the flour, baking powder, sugar, and salt. Stir in the egg and then add the butter. Knead together by hand until smooth. The dough will be quite soft. Shape into a disk, wrap in plastic, and refrigerate for 1 hour.

Preheat the oven to 35-F. Remove the dough & unwrap. Sandwich the dough between 2 pieces of plastic wrap &, using a rolling pin, roll it out to make a circle 11 inches/28cm in diameter. Carefully transfer to a 9-inch/23cm springform pan, pressing the excess dough against the sides of the pan to form a 1-inch/2.5cm edge. You may need to patch the crust here and there due to the dough's softness. Don't worry about overworking the dough. Prep the crust with foil & fill with pie weights/dried beans. Place in the oven & bake for 20 mins.

For filling: Place the sugar and eggs in a bowl & whip together until thick and pale, about 1 minute. Add the cornstarch and salt and mix at medium-low speed until the cornstarch has been absorbed. Add the Quark and sour cream and mix until well combined. Add the vanilla extract, vegetable oil, and milk and mix until well combined.

Remove from the oven & remove the weights &aluminum foil. If the dough has shrunk down from the sides, use the back of a large metal spoon or measuring cup to push it back up again. Scrape the Quark mixture into the hot crust and smooth the top. In all likelihood, the Quark mixture will be higher than the crust you've made. Arrange the mandarin oranges decoratively (in concentric circles, for example) on top of the Quark. Alternatively, scrape half the Quark mixture into the hot crust and smooth. Arrange the drained mandarin oranges on top of the filling and then top with the remaining filling and smooth the top. Return & bake for 65 to 70 minutes, or until the cake is set and the rim of the cake is slightly browned. The cake will still jiggle but should be dry to the touch.

Cool and refrigerate and then serve.

Chocolate Quark Cheesecake

This cheesecake is best if left it to rest for a day before eating and it keeps well, which makes it an ideal make-ahead treat.

Makes: 8 servings

Prep: 1 hr.

Cook: 30 mins

Ingredients:

Crust

- ½ cup sugar
- ⅛ teaspoon salt
- 1 egg
- 1½ cups, minus 1 tablespoon/180g all-purpose flour
- ¼ cup/30g cocoa powder
- 7 tablespoons unsalted high-fat, softened
- ¾ teaspoon baking powder

Filling

- 8½ tablespoons/120g unsalted butter
- 2 cups/500g Quark, drained if necessary (see this page)
- ½ cup plus 2 tablespoons/125g granulated sugar
- 2 eggs
- 2 teaspoons vanilla extract
- 1 tablespoon cornstarch

Directions:

For crust: Beat together the butter & sugar till fluffy. Beat in the egg and scrape down the sides.

In a separate bowl, combine the baking powder, flour, cocoa powder, and salt. With the motor on, add the flour mixture into the butter mixture until well combined. Remove dough onto plastic wrap & form into a disk. It should be soft but not sticky. Wrap it up & refrigerate for 30 mins.

Divide the dough in 1/2 & form each piece into a disk. Wrap one disk in the plastic wrap and return it to the refrigerator. Roll out the second disk between two pieces of plastic wrap until it is approximately 11 inches/28cm in diameter. Remove off the top piece of plastic wrap, and then invert the dough over a 9-inch/23cm springform pan and fit it gently into the pan, removing the plastic wrap as you go. The dough should come up the sides by about 1 inch/2.5cm. Trim any excess and use it to patch any imperfections or set it aside to combine with the remaining dough for the topping. Refrigerate the lined pan while you make the filling.

To make the filling: Heat the oven to 350°F/180°C. Melt the butter. Set aside to cool slightly. Place the Quark in a bowl & whisk in the sugar, either by hand or with an electric mixer. Beat in the eggs & then the cooled butter, vanilla extract, and cornstarch.

When the mixture is creamy and well combined, remove the crust from the refrigerator and pour the filling into the crust. Smooth the top. If necessary, using a knife, trim the sides of the cocoa crust so that it is even all the way around and about ¼ inch/6mm higher than the Quark filling. Reserve any trimmings.

Remove the reserved dough & briefly knead together with any reserved trimmings. Pluck off ½-inch/12mm pieces of the dough and scatter them evenly over the surface of the Quark filling. The pieces of cocoa dough won't sink, but rather will rest on top of the raw filling.

Place in the oven & bake for 45-50 mins. The Quark filling will be golden brown and puffed up.

Remove & let cool on a rack for 20 minutes. After 20 minutes, run a thin knife around the edge of the pan, loosening the cake. Let cool completely before removing the ring. The cake is best if served a day after baking. After it has fully cooled, it can be lightly wrapped in plastic wrap and refrigerated. Serve at room temperature or chilled. The cake will keep well for at least 3 days and up to 1 week in the refrigerator.

Red Velvet Cheesecake

This may take a little more time and effort compared to other dishes and desserts, but it will all be worth it!

Makes: 16 servings

Prep: 3 hrs. 30 mins

Cook: 1 hr. 15 mins

Ingredients:

Cheesecake:

- 2 (8-ounce) packages cream cheese, softened
- ⅔ cup white sugar
- Pinch salt
- ⅓ cup sour cream
- 2 large eggs
- 1 teaspoon vanilla extract
- ⅓ cup heavy whipping cream
- Non-stick cooking spray
- Hot water, for water bath

Red velvet cake:

- 2 ½ cups all-purpose flour
- 1 ½ cups granulated white sugar
- 3 tablespoons unsweetened cocoa powder
- 1 ½ teaspoons baking soda
- 1 teaspoon salt
- 2 large eggs
- 1 ½ cups vegetable oil
- 1 cup buttermilk
- ¼ cup red food coloring
- 2 teaspoons vanilla extract
- 2 teaspoons white vinegar

Frosting:

- 2 ½ cups powdered sugar, sifted
- 2 (8-ounce) packages cream cheese, softened
- ½ cup unsalted butter, softened
- 1 tablespoon vanilla extract

Directions:

Preheat oven to 325F.

Beat the cream cheese, sugar, and salt for about 2 minutes, until creamy and smooth. Add the eggs, mixing again after adding each one. Add the sour cream, heavy cream, and vanilla extract, and beat until smooth and well blended.

Coat a springform pan with baking spray, then place parchment paper on top. Wrap the outsides entirely with two layers of aluminum foil. (This is to prevent water from the water bath from entering the pan.)

Pour the cream cheese batter into the pan, then place it in a pan. Add in the boiling water to the pan to surround the springform pan. Place it in the oven and bake for 45 minutes, until set.

Transfer the springform pan with the cheesecake onto a rack to cool for about 1 hour. Refrigerate overnight.

Preheat oven to 350F.

Combine the flour, sugar, cocoa powder, baking soda, and salt in a large bowl.

In a bowl, mix the eggs, oil, buttermilk, food coloring, vanilla and vinegar. Add the wet ingredients to dry ingredients. Blend for 1 minute with a mixer on medium-low speed, then on high speed for 2 minutes.

Spray non-stick cooking spray in 2 metal baking pans that are the same size as the springform pan used for the cheesecake. Coat the bottoms thinly with flour. Divide the batter between them.

Bake for about 30–35 minutes. The cake is done when only a few crumbs attach to a toothpick when inserted in the center. Transfer the cakes to a rack & let them cool for 10 minutes. Separate the cakes from the pans using a knife around the edges, then invert them onto the rack. Let them cool completely.

To prepare the frosting, mix the powdered sugar, cream cheese, butter, and vanilla using a mixer on medium-high speed, just until smooth.

Assemble the cake by positioning one red velvet cake layer onto a cake plate. Remove the cheesecake from pan, remove parchment paper, and layer it on top of the red velvet cake layer. Top with the second red velvet cake layer.

Coat a thin layer of prepared frosting on the entire outside of the cake. Clean the spatula every time you scoop out from bowl of frosting, so as to not mix crumbs into it. Refrigerate for 30 minutes to set. Then coat cake the with a second layer by adding a large scoop on top then spreading it to the top side of the cake then around it.

Cut into slices. Serve.

Banana Cream Cheesecake

A delicious cheesecake with bananas and vanilla cookies.

Makes: 4 servings

Prep: 20 mins

Cook: 1 hr. 30 mins

Ingredients:

- ¼ cup margarine, melted
- ½ cup whipping cream
- 3 (8-ounce) packages cream cheese, softened
- ⅔ cup sugar
- 20 vanilla sandwich cookies
- 3 eggs
- 2 tablespoons cornstarch
- ¾ cup mashed bananas
- 2 teaspoons vanilla extract

Directions:

Preheat the oven to 350F.

Crush the cookies in either a food processor or blender. When they have turned to crumbs, add the melted butter. Place the mixture in a springform pan and press to entirely cover the bottom and up the sides of the pan. Refrigerate this while you prepare the filling.

Whip cream cheese till smooth, & then add in sugar & corn starch. When the cheese mixture is well blended, add in the eggs one at a time.

When the eggs are incorporated, add the whipping cream, bananas, and vanilla, beating until well combined.

Pour into the springform pan & bake at 350°F for 15 minutes. Reduce the heat to 200°F and bake until the center of the cheesecake is set, about 1 hour and 15 minutes.

When the center is set, remove the cake from the oven. Pop the spring on the pan, but don't remove the sides until the cheesecake has cooled completely. When it is cool, transfer it to the refrigerator. Refrigerate for at least 4 hours before serving.

Serve with whipped cream and freshly sliced bananas.

White Chocolate Cheesecake

This make-ahead cake is absolutely sinful. The combination of chocolate and cheese raises the simple cheesecake to gourmet heights. If the cake or cookie crumbs are not chocolate, you must add dried cocoa.

Makes: 8 servings

Prep: 10 mins

Cook: 40 mins

Ingredients:

Crust

- 1½ cups dried chocolate cake or cookie crumbs
- 1 tablespoon cocoa powder (if crumbs are not chocolate)
- 2½ tablespoons margarine or butter, melted

Filling

- 1 cup cottage cheese
- One 8-ounce package cream cheese, softened
- 3 eggs
- 1 cup sugar
- 1 tablespoon lemon juice
- 2 tablespoons rice flour
- 3 squares white baking chocolate, melted

Directions:

Preheat oven to 375F.

Crust: Tumble together the crumbs, cocoa (if using), and butter. Pat into the bottom of a 9" pie plate or 8" springform pan, reserving 2 tablespoons for sprinkling on top (if desired).

Filling: Whip cottage cheese in a blender or mixer until smooth and creamy. Add the cream cheese, eggs, sugar, lemon juice, and flour. Beat thoroughly. Stir in the chocolate. Pour into the crust and scatter on the reserved crumbs (if desired). Bake for 35 to 40 minutes, or until set.

Refrigerate for several hours before serving.

Black Forest Cheesecake

An easy-to-make, eye-appealing, and delicious cheesecake with all the flavors of the cake from which it takes its name. If the cake or cookie crumbs are not chocolate, add dried cocoa.

Makes: 12 servings

Prep: 10 mins

Cook: 40 mins

Ingredients:

Crust

- 1½ cup dried chocolate cake or cookie crumbs
- 1 tablespoon cocoa powder (if crumbs are not chocolate)
- 3 tablespoons butter or margarine, melted

Cake

- Two 8-ounce packages cream cheese, softened
- 1 cup cottage cheese
- 4 eggs
- 1 cup sugar
- ½ cup semisweet chocolate chips
- ½ cup maraschino cherries, drained and chopped

Directions:

Preheat oven to 375°.

Combine the crumbs, cocoa (if using), and butter. Pat into a 10" springform pan.

In a bowl, whip the cream cheese, cottage cheese, eggs, and sugar until well blended and smooth. Stir in the chocolate chips, and cherries. Pour gently into the crust. Bake for 35-40 mins/until the center is set.

When cool, put in fridge overnight, before serving.

Ricotta Pineapple Cheesecake

A fruited cheesecake with fewer calories but still as delicious!

Makes: 8 servings

Prep: 10 mins

Cook: 40 mins

Ingredients:

Crust

- 1¼ cups cookie crumbs
- ¼ cup ground almonds
- 3 tablespoons margarine or butter, melted

Filling

- 3 eggs, separated
- One 15-ounce container ricotta cheese
- 1 cup sugar
- 2 tablespoons cornstarch
- 1 teaspoon dried orange peel
- One 8½-ounce can crushed pineapple, drained

Directions:

Preheat oven to 375F

Crust: Mix together the crumbs, nuts, and margarine. Pat into an 8" springform pan or a 9" pie plate.

Filling: Beat the egg whites till stiff. In a bowl, whip together the ricotta cheese, egg yolks, sugar, cornstarch, and orange peel. Stir in the pineapple. Gently fold in the beaten egg whites. Pour into the crust. Bake for approximately 40 mins. Serve warm or cool.

Fruit Cheesecake Pie

Fresh fruit in season plus a cheesecake custard topping make this a rich, mouth-watering dessert for a crowd. Change the flavor with your choice of fruits—spring rhubarb, winter apples, local cherries, or exotic pineapple. You should refrigerate the pie at least two hours or longer before serving.

Makes: 10 servings

Prep: 30 mins

Cook: 30 mins

Ingredients:

Fruit Layer

- 3 cups fresh fruit (cherries, rhubarb, pineapple, etc.)
- 1 tablespoon water
- 1 cup sugar
- 2 tablespoons cornstarch
- 1 teaspoon flavored gelatin, for color

Cheesecake Topping

- Two 3-ounce packages cream cheese, softened
- 2 eggs
- 1 tablespoon lemon juice
- 6 tablespoons sugar
- 1 cup sour cream or nondairy substitute

Directions:

Preheat oven to 350F.

Prepare the crust (reserving 2 tablespoons of the mixture). Do not bake.

Prepare the fruit by cutting the rhubarb into ½-inch slices, pitting the cherries or peeling, coring, and cutting the pineapple into small (½ inch or less) tidbits.

In a 2-quart saucepan, mix together the selected fruit, the water, sugar, and cornstarch. (Eliminate the water if the fruit is very juicy.) Cook, stirring often over medium heat, until the mixture comes to a full boil. Remove from heat and add the gelatin (raspberry for rhubarb, cherry for cherry, and lemon for apple and pineapple). Pour the fruit mixture in prepared crust.

With a mixer, blend together the cream cheese, eggs, lemon juice, sugar, and sour cream. Pour over the fruit filling. Top with a sprinkling of the reserved crumb mix.

Bake for 25 to 30 minutes, or until the center appears set when shaken gently.

Cool and then refrigerate from 2 to 24 hours before serving.

White Chocolate Oreo Cheesecake

A delicious Oreo and white chocolate cheesecake recipe.

Makes: 12 servings

Prep: 5 hrs.

Cook: 45 mins

Ingredients:

- 21 chocolate sandwich cookies (from an 8-ounce package)
- 6 ounces white chocolate
- 32 ounces (four 8-ounce packages) cream cheese, at room temperature
- 1 cup granulated sugar
- 2 tablespoons cornstarch
- 1 cup sour cream
- 2 teaspoons pure vanilla extract
- 4 large eggs

Directions:

Preheat the oven to 350°F. Set aside a 9-inch springform pan.

Break 9 of the cookies in half and place them in a food processor. Pulse the cookies until crumbly, about 15 times. You should have 1¼ cups of cookie crumbs. Place the cookie crumbs in the bottom of the springform pan and distribute them evenly with your fingers. The crumbs may thinly cover the bottom of the pan. Set the pan with the chocolate crumb crust aside.

Break the white chocolate in 1-inch pieces & place them in an 8-ounce microwave-safe container. Microwave the chocolate for 20-30 seconds, remove it from the microwave, & add it until the chocolate has melted. Set the white chocolate aside to cool.

Place the cream cheese & sugar in a large mixing bowl and beat with an electric mixer on low speed till the sugar is incorporated, about 20 seconds. Increase the mixer speed to medium and beat the cream cheese mixture until creamy, about 1½ minutes. Stop the machine and add the cornstarch, sour cream, cooled white chocolate, and the vanilla. Beat on low speed until combined, about 30 seconds. Add the eggs, beating on low speed until each is just combined. Set the cheesecake batter aside.

Place 11 of the cookies on a cutting board and coarsely chop them. You should have about 1½ cups of chopped cookies. Fold the chopped cookies into the cheesecake batter.

Place the springform pan on a baking sheet. Pour the cheesecake batter over the chocolate crumb crust and smooth the top with a rubber spatula. Place in oven & let the cheesecake bake until it is golden brown around the edges but still a slight jiggly in the center, 45 mins. Turn off the oven, leaving it in for 2 hours to set.

At the end of the 2 hrs., remove the pan from the oven and let the cheesecake cool to room temperature for about 1 hour. Cover the top of the cheesecake pan with plastic wrap and place the pan in the fridge for the cheesecake to chill for at least 4 hrs.

To serve, remove the side of the springform pan. Place the cheesecake, still attached to the bottom of the pan, on a serving plate. Divide the remaining chocolate sandwich cookie in half and garnish the center of the cheesecake with the cookie halves. Slice and serve.

Blue Velvet Cheesecake

Prefer blue velvet to red velvet? We've got you covered!

Makes: 16 servings

Prep: 3 hrs. 30 mins

Cook: 1 hr. 15 mins

Ingredients:

Cheesecake:

- 2 (8-ounce) packages cream cheese, softened
- ⅔ cup white sugar
- Pinch salt
- ⅓ cup sour cream
- 2 large eggs
- 1 teaspoon vanilla extract
- ⅓ cup heavy whipping cream
- Non-stick cooking spray
- Hot water, for water bath

Blue velvet cake:

- 2 ½ cups all-purpose flour
- 1 ½ cups granulated white sugar
- 3 tablespoons unsweetened cocoa powder
- 1 ½ teaspoons baking soda
- 1 teaspoon salt
- 2 large eggs
- 1 ½ cups vegetable oil
- 1 cup buttermilk
- ¼ cup red food coloring
- 2 teaspoons vanilla extract
- 2 teaspoons white vinegar

Frosting:

- 2 ½ cups powdered sugar, sifted
- 2 (8-ounce) packages cream cheese, softened
- ½ cup unsalted butter, softened
- 1 tablespoon vanilla extract

Directions:

Preheat oven to 325F.

Beat the cream cheese, sugar, and salt for about 2 minutes, until creamy and smooth. Add the eggs, mixing again after adding each one. Add the sour cream, heavy cream, and vanilla extract, and beat until smooth and well blended.

Coat a springform pan with baking spray, then place parchment paper on top. Wrap the outsides entirely with two layers of aluminum foil. (This is to prevent water from the water bath from entering the pan.)

Pour the cream cheese batter into the pan, then place it in a pan. Add in the boiling water to the pan to surround the springform pan. Place it in the oven and bake for 45 minutes, until set.

Transfer the springform pan with the cheesecake onto a rack to cool for about 1 hour. Refrigerate overnight.

Preheat oven to 350F.

Combine the flour, sugar, cocoa powder, baking soda, and salt in a large bowl.

In a bowl, mix the eggs, oil, buttermilk, food coloring, vanilla and vinegar. Add the wet ingredients to dry ingredients. Blend for 1 minute with a mixer on medium-low speed, then on high speed for 2 minutes.

Spray non-stick cooking spray in 2 metal baking pans that are the same size as the springform pan used for the cheesecake. Coat the bottoms thinly with flour. Divide the batter between them.

Bake for about 30–35 minutes. The cake is done when only a few crumbs attach to a toothpick when inserted in the center. Transfer the cakes to a rack & let them cool for 10 minutes. Separate the cakes from the pans using a knife around the edges, then invert them onto the rack. Let them cool completely.

To prepare the frosting, mix the powdered sugar, cream cheese, butter, and vanilla using a mixer on medium-high speed, just until smooth.

Assemble the cake by positioning one cake layer onto a cake plate. Remove the cheesecake from pan, remove parchment paper, and layer it on top of the blue velvet cake layer. Top with the second cake layer.

Coat a thin layer of prepared frosting on the entire outside of the cake. Clean the spatula every time you scoop out from bowl of frosting, so as to not mix crumbs into it. Refrigerate for 30 minutes to set. Then coat cake the with a second layer by adding a large scoop on top then spreading it to the top side of the cake then around it.

Cut into slices. Serve.

Peaches and Cream Cheesecake

A fruity and delicious cheesecake with peaches.

Makes: 8 servings

Prep: 10 mins

Cook: 40 mins

Ingredients:

Crust

- 1¼ cups cookie crumbs
- ¼ cup ground almonds
- 3 tablespoons margarine or butter, melted

Filling

- 3 eggs, separated
- One 15-ounce container ricotta cheese
- 1 cup sugar
- 2 tablespoons cornstarch
- 1 teaspoon dried orange peel
- One 8½-ounce can crushed peaches, drained

Directions:

Preheat oven to 375F

Crust: Mix together the crumbs, nuts, and margarine. Pat into an 8" springform pan or a 9" pie plate.

Filling: Beat the egg whites till stiff. In a bowl, whip together the ricotta cheese, egg yolks, sugar, cornstarch, and orange peel. Stir in the peaches. Gently fold in the beaten egg whites. Pour into the crust. Bake for approximately 40 mins. Serve warm or cool.

Matcha Cheesecake

Matcha lovers will love this delicious cheesecake recipe!

Makes: 12 servings

Prep: 4 hrs. 15 mins

Cook: 1 hr. 5 mins

Ingredients:

Crust:

- ⅓ cup margarine, melted
- ¼ teaspoon ground cinnamon
- 1 ½ cups graham cracker crumbs

Filling:

- 2 teaspoons vanilla extract
- 2 tsp matcha powder
- 5 large eggs
- 1 ¼ cups white sugar
- 4 (8-ounce) packages cream cheese, softened
- ½ cup sour cream

Directions:

Preheat oven to 475F & place a skillet with half an inch of water inside.

Combine the ingredients for crust in a bowl. Line a large pie pan with parchment paper and spread crust onto pan. Press firmly. Cover it with foil & keep it in the freezer until ready to use.

Combine all for filling apart from the eggs in a bowl. . Mix in eggs 1 at a time & beat until fully blended.

Remove the crust & pour in the filling, spreading it evenly. Place the pie pan into the heated skillet in the oven and bake for about 12 minutes.

Reduce the heat to 350°F. Continue to bake for about 50 minutes, or until the top of the cake is golden. Remove it from the oven & move the skillet onto a wire rack to cool.

Refrigerate for at least 4 hours.

Serve cold.

Lavender Cheesecake

A fancy cheesecake recipe for when you want to impress your guests!

Makes: 12 servings

Prep: 4 hrs. 15 mins

Cook: 1 hr. 5 mins

Ingredients:

Crust:

- ⅓ cup margarine, melted
- ¼ teaspoon ground cinnamon
- 1 ½ cups graham cracker crumbs

Filling:

- 2 teaspoons vanilla extract
- 4 (8-ounce) packages cream cheese, softened
- ½ cup sour cream
- 1 tbsp. lavender, chopped
- 1 ¼ cups white sugar
- 5 large eggs

Directions:

Preheat oven to 475F & place a skillet with half an inch of water inside.

Combine the ingredients for crust in a bowl. Line a large pie pan with parchment paper and spread crust onto pan. Press firmly. Cover it with foil & keep it in the freezer until ready to use.

Combine all for filling apart from the eggs in a bowl. . Mix in eggs 1 at a time & beat until fully blended.

Remove the crust & pour in the filling, spreading it evenly. Place the pie pan into the heated skillet in the oven and bake for about 12 minutes.

Reduce the heat to 350°F. Continue to bake for about 50 minutes, or until the top of the cake is golden. Remove it from the oven & move the skillet onto a wire rack to cool.

Refrigerate for at least 4 hours.

Serve cold.

Mango Cheesecake

A delicious and tropical cheesecake recipe that's best when ripe mangoes are used!

Makes: 12 servings

Prep: 4 hrs. 15 mins

Cook: 1 hr. 5 mins

Ingredients:

Crust:

- ⅓ cup margarine, melted
- ¼ teaspoon ground cinnamon
- 1 ½ cups graham cracker crumbs

Filling:

- 1 ¼ cups white sugar
- 4 (8-ounce) packages cream cheese, softened
- 2 cups mango puree
- ½ cup sour cream
- 5 large eggs
- 2 teaspoons vanilla extract

Directions:

Preheat oven to 475F & place a skillet with half an inch of water inside.

Combine the ingredients for crust in a bowl. Line a large pie pan with parchment paper and spread crust onto pan. Press firmly. Cover it with foil & keep it in the freezer until ready to use.

Combine all for filling apart from the eggs in a bowl. . Mix in eggs 1 at a time & beat until fully blended.

Remove the crust & pour in the filling, spreading it evenly. Place the pie pan into the heated skillet in the oven and bake for about 12 minutes.

Reduce the heat to 350°F. Continue to bake for about 50 minutes, or until the top of the cake is golden. Remove it from the oven & move the skillet onto a wire rack to cool.

Refrigerate for at least 4 hours.

Serve cold.

Caramel Cheesecake

An amazing, indulgent caramel cheesecake recipe that everyone will love!

Makes: 12 servings

Prep: 4 hrs. 15 mins

Cook: 1 hr. 5 mins

Ingredients:

Crust:

- ⅓ cup margarine, melted
- ¼ teaspoon ground cinnamon
- 1 ½ cups graham cracker crumbs

Filling:

- 2 teaspoons vanilla extract
- 4 (8-ounce) packages cream cheese, softened
- ½ cup sour cream
- 5 large eggs
- 1 cup Dulce de Leche
- 1 ¼ cups white sugar

Directions:

Preheat oven to 475F & place a skillet with half an inch of water inside.

Combine the ingredients for crust in a bowl. Line a large pie pan with parchment paper and spread crust onto pan. Press firmly. Cover it with foil & keep it in the freezer until ready to use.

Combine all for filling apart from the eggs in a bowl. . Mix in eggs 1 at a time & beat until fully blended.

Remove the crust & pour in the filling, spreading it evenly. Place the pie pan into the heated skillet in the oven and bake for about 12 minutes.

Reduce the heat to 350°F. Continue to bake for about 50 minutes, or until the top of the cake is golden. Remove it from the oven & move the skillet onto a wire rack to cool.

Refrigerate for at least 4 hours.

Serve cold.

Chocolate Mocha Cheesecake

Coffee and chocolate come together to make this delicious, to-die-for cheesecake!

Makes: 8 – 12 servings

Prep: 15 mins

Cook: 1 hr. plus cooling time

Ingredients:

For the Crust:

- 12 Oreo cookies, crushed, plus extra to serve
- 1 tbsp. white sugar
- 2 tbsp. unsalted butter, melted

For the Filling:

- 4 tbsp. milk
- 1 cup semisweet chocolate chips
- 3 tsp. espresso powder
- 12 oz. cream cheese, softened
- 1/2 cup white sugar
- 2 large eggs
- ½ tsp. vanilla extract
- 1 tbsp. flour

Directions:

Preheat the oven to 375F & slightly grease a 6"inch springform pan.

For the Crust: In a medium-sized bowl, combine the crushed Oreos, sugar & melted butter. Press the crumb mixture in pan & bake for 10 minutes. Remove & set aside to slightly cool.

Reduce the oven to 350°F.

For filling: In a saucepan, combine the milk and chocolate chips and heat on low until the chocolate chips are melted. Remove from heat and add in the espresso powder. Set the mixture aside.

In a large bowl, beat together the cream cheese and sugar for about 2 minutes. Add in the eggs & beat again until well-combined. Finally, add in the vanilla extract and flour and beat until well-combined.

Pour batter onto the crust and bake for about 45 minutes.

Turn off & leave the door open several inches and leave to cool for about an hour.

Remove, cover and cool in the refrigerator for another hour or until ready to serve.

Top with crushed Oreos and serve.

Enjoy!

Caramel Coffee Cheesecake

Creamy Dulce de leche and espresso powder come together to give you a heavenly cheesecake recipe!

Makes: 12 servings

Prep: 4 hrs. 15 mins

Cook: 1 hr. 5 mins

Ingredients:

Crust:

- ⅓ cup margarine, melted
- ¼ teaspoon ground cinnamon
- 1 ½ cups graham cracker crumbs

Filling:

- 2 teaspoons vanilla extract
- 4 (8-ounce) packages cream cheese, softened
- ½ cup sour cream
- 1 cup Dulce de Leche
- 5 large eggs
- 3 tsp espresso powder
- 1 ¼ cups white sugar

Directions:

Preheat oven to 475F & place a skillet with half an inch of water inside.

Combine the ingredients for crust in a bowl. Line a large pie pan with parchment paper and spread crust onto pan. Press firmly. Cover it with foil & keep it in the freezer until ready to use.

Combine all for filling apart from the eggs in a bowl. . Mix in eggs 1 at a time & beat until fully blended.

Remove the crust & pour in the filling, spreading it evenly. Place the pie pan into the heated skillet in the oven and bake for about 12 minutes.

Reduce the heat to 350°F. Continue to bake for about 50 minutes, or until the top of the cake is golden. Remove it from the oven & move the skillet onto a wire rack to cool.

Refrigerate for at least 4 hours.

Serve cold.

Conclusion

Well, there you have it! Delicious cheesecake recipes for you to try out at home! Make sure you give each cheesecake flavor a try and don't forget to share them with your friends and family!

About the Author

Allie Allen developed her passion for the culinary arts at the tender age of five when she would help her mother cook for their large family of 8. Even back then, her family knew this would be more than a hobby for the young Allie and when she graduated from high school, she applied to cooking school in London. It had always been a dream of the young chef to study with some of Europe's best and she made it happen by attending the Chef Academy of London.

After graduation, Allie decided to bring her skills back to North America and open up her own restaurant. After 10 successful years as head chef and owner, she decided to sell her business and pursue other career avenues. This monumental decision led Allie to her true calling, teaching. She also started to write e-books for her students to study at home for practice. She is now the proud author of several e-books and gives private and semi-private cooking lessons to a range of students at all levels of experience.

Stay tuned for more from this dynamic chef and teacher when she releases more informative e-books on cooking and baking in the near future. Her work is infused with stores and anecdotes you will love!

Author's Afterthoughts

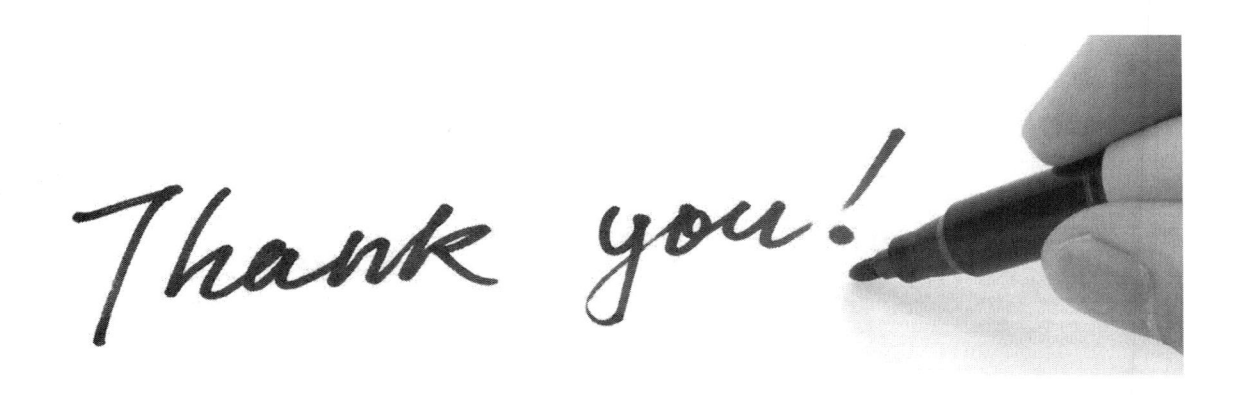

I can't tell you how grateful I am that you decided to read my book. My most heartfelt thanks that you took time out of your life to choose my work and I hope you find benefit within these pages.

There are so many books available today that offer similar content so that makes it even more humbling that you decided to buying mine.

Tell me what you thought! I am eager to hear your opinion and ideas on what you read as are others who are looking for a good book to buy. Leave a review on Amazon.com so others can benefit from your wisdom!

With much thanks,

Allie Allen

Printed in Great Britain
by Amazon